Sales Mastery

GEMS MASTERY SERIES

SIMPLE SALES IDEAS GUARANTEED TO INCREASE YOUR BOTTOM LINE!

Quotes Compiled & Edited

by

DeCarlo A. Eskridge

NU DAE Enterprise Publications

United States of America

ISBN-13: 978-1469912424
ISBN-10: 1469912422

Edited by DeCarlo A.. Eskridge
Cover Design ©NU DAE Enterprises, LLC, 2012
DeCarloEskridge.com

Printed in the United States of America

To the
memory of
my mother

Acknowledgments

Jesus (1), Robert Heinlein (2), Sidney Madwed (3), O. B. Smith (4) Bob Hooey (5), Jim Rohn (6, 30, 74), Nelson Boswell (7), Sam Walton (8), Alice Macdougall (9), Ray Kroc (10), John D. Rockefeller (11), Graham Day (12), W. Clement Stone (13), Gene Buckley (14), Zig Ziglar (15, 44, 93, 112), Mark Twain (16), Shiv Singh (17), Napoleon Hill (18), Tom Watson (19), Aristotle (20, 111), C.F. Norton (21), Arnold H. Glasgow (22), Bo Bennett (24, 49, 124), Henry Ward Beecher (25), Robert Schuller (26), Thomas Edison (27), Larry D. Turner (28), Heraclitus (29), Nikos Kazantzakis (31), Patricia Fripp (32, 71), Robert Louis Stevenson (33), Estée Lauder (34), Curtis Carlson (35), Kees Kamies (36), Frank Zappa (37), Don Marquis (38), Roy Bartell (40), DeCarlo Eskridge (41, 99, 110), George Matthew Adams (42), Elbert Hubbard (43), Mary Kay Ash (45), Frank Lloyd Wright (46), John Mason (47), Dennis R. Kyle (48), Henry A. Kissinger (50), Orville Redenbacher (51), Debbi Fields (52), Albert Einstein (53), J.G. Holland (54), Shane Gibson (55), David Ogilvy (56), Michael Jordan (57), Martin Luther King, Jr. (58), Louis Lundborg (59) Lou Holtz (60), Ben Feldman (61), Alexis de Tocqueville (62), R. H. Grant (63), Paul J. Meyer (64), Harvey MacKay (65), Bob Burg (66), Malcolm Forbes (67), Tom Hopkins (69), Nicholas Sparks (70), Ronnie Milsap (72), Rosser Reeves (73), Joe Paterno (75), Les Brown (76), A. J. Foyt (77), Oprah Winfrey (78), Brian Tracy (79), Ronald E. Osborn (80), Paul Bryant (81), Ancient Samurai Proverb (82), Abraham H. Maslow (83), Dwight D. Eisenhower (84, 106), Conrad Hilton (85), Kate Zabriskic (86), Jean-Claude Kelly (87), Vincent T. Lombardi (88), Amos Parrish (89), Tommy Lasorda (90),

George C. Hubbs (91), Jeffrey Gitomer (94), Terry Pratchett (95), Gilbert K. Chesterton (96), Victor Cherbuliez (97), Bob Moawad (98), Henry Van Dyke (100), Jack Schwartz (101), Wayne Dyer (102), Al Neuharth (103), Damon Richards (104), Jim Fox (105), Eleanor Roosevelt (107), Soichiro Honda (108), Martina Navratilova (109), Calvin Coolidge (113), Emily Post (114), Josh Billings (115), Edward Said (116), Robert Keith Leavitt (117), Helen Keller (118), Jalal Uddin Rumi (119), Nick Gleason (120), Og Mandino (121), Mark Shuttleworth (122), Peter Sotos (123), Charles Michael Schwab (125)

Introduction

Are great salespeople born or are they made great? Can anyone learn to be a more effective salesperson? The truth is you do not need 20 years of experience, formal training, or a degree from an Ivy League University to be a more effective salesperson.

Ask any qualified sales manager with more than a few years experience, if they have ever known a salesperson with no natural talents who succeeded wildly, simply because they were disciplined, focused, and relentless. No doubt, they will have names and stories. We are all in the business of selling. Anytime you try to influence someone's thoughts or actions, you are selling. Top-notch salespeople understand in order to succeed in sales; they are responsible for developing the skills needed for sales mastery.

In this book, you will discover timeless gems (*quotes*) from some of the world's most influential sales leaders. Leaders and innovators, who have turned their values into action and, in the process, changed the way the world does business. **Sales Mastery** should be must reading for everyone in the field of sales and/or those who support those in sales. In order to get the most from your reading, we recommend that you read this book until you master the precious gems within.

$\mathcal{A}$sk and it will be given to you; seek and you will find; knock and the door will be opened to you. For everyone who asks receives; the one who seeks finds; and to the one who knocks, the door will be opened.

- Jesus

♦

$\mathcal{L}$isten to the experts.
They'll tell you
what can't be done
and why.
Then do it.

- Robert Heinlein

♦

Everyone is in business for himself, for he is selling his services, labor or ideas. Until one realizes that this is true he will not take conscious charge of his life and will always be looking outside himself for guidance.

- **Sidney Madwed**

◆

$\mathcal{C}$onfidence
and enthusiasm are the
greatest sales producers in
any kind of economy.

- O. B. Smith

◆

$\mathcal{I}$f you are not taking care of your customer, your competitor will.

- Bob Hooey

♦

$\mathcal{T}$o succeed in sales, simply talk to lots of people every day. And here's what's exciting – there are lots of people!

- Jim Rohn

♦

*H*ere is a simple but powerful rule: always give people more than what they expect to get.

- Nelson Boswell

◆

The goal as a company is to have customer service that is not just the best but legendary.

- Sam Walton

◆

In business you get what you want by giving other people what they want.

- Alice Macdougall

◆

If you work just for money, you'll never make it. But if you love what you are doing, and always put the customer first, success will be yours.

- Ray Kroc

♦

$\mathcal{I}$ do not think there is any other quality so essential to success of any kind as the quality of perseverance. It overcomes almost everything, even nature.

- John D. Rockefeller

♦

$\mathcal{I}$f you love your customer to death, you can't go wrong.

- Graham Day

Sale are contingent upon the attitude of the salesman, not the attitude of the prospect.

- W. Clement Stone

♦

Don't try to tell the customer what he wants. If you want to be smart, be smart in the shower. Then get out, go to work and serve the customer!

- **Gene Buckley**

♦

$\mathcal{F}$or every sale you miss because you're too enthusiastic, you will miss a hundred because you're not enthusiastic enough.

- Zig Ziglar

$\mathcal{T}$wenty years from now you will be more disappointed by the things you didn't do than by the ones you did do.
So throw off the bowlines. Sail away from the safe harbor. Catch the trade winds in your sails. Explore. Dream. Discover.

- Mark Twain

♦

The purpose of a business is to create a customer who creates customers.

- Shiv Singh

♦

One of the most important principles of success is developing the habit of going the extra mile.

- Napoleon Hill

◆

$\mathcal{O}$f you don't genuinely like your customers, chances are they won't buy.

- Tom Watson

◆

We are what we repeatedly do. Excellence, then, is not an act, but a habit.

- **Aristotle**

◆

$\mathcal{N}$othing is ever gained by winning an argument and losing a customer.

- C.F. Norton

♦

Success isn't a result of spontaneous combustion. You must set yourself on fire.

- Arnold H. Glasgow

◆

You have to do what others won't. To achieve what others don't.
- **Anonymous**

◆

In sales, a referral is the key to the door of resistance.

- Bo Bennett

$\mathscr{I}$ never knew an early-rising, hard-working, prudent man, careful of his earnings, and strictly honest who complained of bad luck.

- Henry Ward Beecher

◆

I will! I am! I can! I will actualize my dream. I will press ahead. I will settle down and see it through. I will solve the problems. I will pay the price. I will never walk away from my dream until I see my dream walk away: Alert! Alive! Achieved!

- Robert Schuller

♦

$\mathcal{I}$f we did the things we are capable of, we would astound ourselves.

- Thomas Edison

On any given Monday I am one sale closer and one idea away from being a Millionaire.

- Larry D. Turner

♦

Day by day, what you do
is who you become.

- Heraclitus

♦

*F*ormal education will make you a living; self-education will make you a fortune.

- Jim Rohn

♦

$\mathscr{I}$n order to succeed, we must first believe that we can.

- Nikos Kazantzakis

You don't close a sale, you open a relationship if you want to build a long-term, successful enterprise.

- Patricia Fripp

♦

$\mathcal{E}$veryone lives by selling something.

- Robert Louis Stevenson

◆

$\mathcal{I}$ have never worked a day in my life without selling. If I believe in something, I sell it, and I sell it hard.

- **Estée Lauder**

♦

$\mathcal{Y}$ou've got to be success minded. You've got to feel that things are coming your way when you're out selling; otherwise, you won't be able to sell anything.

- **Curtis Carlson**

◆

Give trust, and you'll get it double in return.

- Kees Kamies

Art is making something out of nothing and selling it.

- Frank Zappa

◆

The successful people are the ones who can think up things for the rest of the world to keep busy at.

- Don Marquis

♦

To my customer.
I may not have the answer,
but I'll find it.
I may not have the time,
but I'll make it.

- Anonymous

◆

Most people think "selling" is the same as "talking". But the most effective salespeople know that listening is the most important part of their job.

- Roy Bartell

◆

$\mathcal{T}$he goal of sales training is to train people how to serve clients in an extraordinary fashion.

- DeCarlo Eskridge

◆

There is no such thing as a self-made man. We are made up of thousands of others. Everyone who has ever done a kind deed for us, or spoken one word of encouragement to us, has entered into the makeup of our character and our thoughts, as well as our success.

- George Matthew Adams

♦

$\mathcal{M}$en are rich only as they give. He who gives great service gets great rewards.

- Elbert Hubbard

◆

$\mathcal{E}$very sale has five basic obstacles: no need, no money, no hurry, no desire, no trust.

- Zig Ziglar

♦

$\mathcal{A}$ mediocre idea that generates enthusiasm will go further than a great idea that inspires no one.

- Mary Kay Ash

♦

$\mathcal{B}$usiness is like riding a bicycle. Either you keep moving or you fall down.

- Frank Lloyd Wright

◆

$\mathcal{T}$he most unprofitable
item ever manufactured is
an excuse.

- John Mason

♦

$\mathcal{C}$onsistency is a critical key to your success in sales. Whether you are making telephone calls, visiting clients, or direct marketing you have to hit your numbers everyday. A consistent sales work ethic will make you more successful than the sporadic every third day over-achiever hands down.

- Dennis R. Kyle

◆

$\mathcal{I}$ like to think of sales as
the ability to gracefully
persuade, not manipulate, a
person or persons into a
win-win situation.

- Bo Bennett

◆

$\mathcal{O}$f eighty percent of your sales come from twenty percent of all of your items, just carry those twenty percent.

- Henry A. Kissinger

◆

We got to know the competition very well. In the '50s popcorn made a big growth in sales. Our main push was to produce the best quality and sell in quality retail outlets.

- Orville Redenbacher

♦

You do not have to be superhuman to do what you believe in.

- Debbi Fields

♦

$\mathscr{S}$etting an example is not the main means of influencing others; it is the only means.

- Albert Einstein

◆

The secret of man's success resides in his insight into the moods of people, and his fact in dealing with them.

- J. G. Holland

♦

$\mathcal{A}$lways be closing… that doesn't mean you're always closing the deal, but it does mean that you need to be always closing on the next step in the process.

- Shane Gibson

◆

I never tell one client that I cannot attend his sales convention because I have a previous engagement with another client; successful polygamy depends upon pretending to each spouse that she is the only pebble on your beach.

- David Ogilvy

♦

$\mathcal{I}$’ve failed over and over again in my life. And that is why I succeed.

- Michael Jordan

◆

$\mathcal{L}$ife's most persistent
and urgent question is,
"What are you doing for
others?"

- Martin Luther King, Jr.

◆

$\mathcal{S}$uccess –

my nomination for the
single most important
ingredient is energy well
directed.

- Louis Lundborg

Show me someone who has done something worthwhile, and I'll show you someone who has overcome adversity.

- Lou Holtz

♦

$\mathcal{D}$on't sell life insurance.
Sell what life insurance
can do.

- Ben Feldman

♦

$\mathcal{W}$e succeed
in enterprises which
demand the positive
qualities we possess,
but we excel in those
which can also make use
of our defects.

- Alexis de Tocqueville

◆

$\mathcal{A}$ salesman, like the storage battery in your car, is constantly discharging energy. Unless he is recharged at frequent intervals he soon runs dry. This is one of the greatest responsibilities of sales leadership.

- R. H. Grant

♦

*F*orget about the business outlook, be on the outlook for business.

- Paul J. Meyer

♦

The sale begins when the customer says yes.

- Harvey MacKay

♦

$\mathcal{I}$nternalize the Golden Rule of sales that says: All things being equal, people will do business with, and refer business to, those people they know, like and trust.

- Bob Burg

◆

$\mathcal{V}$ictory is sweetest
when you've known
defeat.

- Malcolm Forbes

◆

$\mathscr{A}$ smart salesperson
listens to emotions not just
facts.

- Anonymous

♦

$\mathcal{I}$n sales there are going to be times when you can't make everyone happy. Don't expect to and you won't be disappointed. Just do your best for each client in each situation as it arises. Then, learn from each situation how to do it better the next time.

- Tom Hopkins

◆

$\mathcal{A}$bove all, a query letter is a sales pitch and it is the single most important page an unpublished writer will ever write. It's the first impression and will either open the door or close it. It's that important, so don't mess it up. Mine took 17 drafts and two weeks to write.

- **Nicholas Sparks**

♦

It is not your customer's job to remember you. It is your obligation and responsibility to make sure they don't have the chance to forget you.

- Patricia Fripp

♦

$\mathcal{W}$ork for the fun of it,
and the money will arrive
some day.

- Ronnie Milsap

◆

$\mathcal{A}$dvertising is, actually, a simple phenomenon in terms of economics. It is merely a substitute for a personal sales force - an extension, if you will, of the merchant who cries aloud his wares.

- Rosser Reeves

◆

You don't get paid for the hour. You get paid for the value you bring to the hour.

- Jim Rohn

♦

$\mathscr{Y}$ou have to perform at a consistently higher level than others. That's the mark of a true professional.

- **Joe Paterno**

♦

You gotta be hungry!

- Les Brown

You get out in front -
you stay out in front.

- A. J. Foyt

◆

$\mathcal{R}$eal integrity is doing the right thing, knowing that nobody's going to know whether you did it or not.

- Oprah Winfrey

◆

Remember, you only
have to succeed the last
time.

- Brian Tracy

♦

$\mathcal{U}$nless you try to do something beyond what you have already mastered, you will never grow.

- Ronald E. Osborn

Show class, have pride, and display character. If you do, winning takes care of itself.

- Paul Bryant

♦

Warriors take chances. Like everyone else, they fear failing, but they refuse to let fear control them.

- Ancient Samurai Proverb

◆

$\mathcal{W}$e are not in a position in which we have nothing to work with. We already have capacities, talents, direction, missions, and callings.

- Abraham H. Maslow

◆

What counts is not necessarily the size of the dog in the fight - it's the size of the fight in the dog.

- Dwight D. Eisenhower

Success seems to be connected with action. Successful people keep moving. They make mistakes, but they don't quit.

- Conrad Hilton

The customer's
perception is your reality.

- Kate Zabriskie

$\mathcal{T}$he best and fastest way to learn … is to watch and imitate a champion.

- Jean-Claude Kelly

◆

$\mathcal{T}$he difference between a successful person and others is not a lack of strength, not a lack of knowledge, but rather a lack of will.

- Vincent T. Lombardi

♦

*T*he best leaders are those most interested in surrounding themselves with assistants and associates smarter than they are. They are frank in admitting this and are willing to pay for such talents.

- Amos Parrish

◆

The difference between the impossible and the possible lies in a person's determination.

- **Tommy Lasorda**

◆

$\mathscr{I}$f your work is becoming uninteresting, so are you. Work is an inanimate thing and can be made lively and interesting only by injecting yourself into it. Your job is only as big as you are.

- George C. Hubbs

◆

Of Columbus had turned back, no one would have blamed him. Of course, no one would have remembered him either.

- Anonymous

♦

Timid salesmen have
skinny kids.

- Zig Ziglar

♦

The key is not to call the decision maker. The key is to have the decision maker call you.

- Jeffrey Gitomer

◆

Only in our dreams are
we free. The rest of the
time we need wages.

- Terry Pratchett

♦

*H*ow you think when you lose determines how long it will be until you win.

- Gilbert K. Chesterton

◆

What helps luck is a habit of watching for opportunities, of having a patient but restless mind, of sacrificing one's ease or vanity, or uniting a love of detail to foresight, and of passing through hard times bravely and cheerfully.

- Victor Cherbuliez

♦

Quality begins on the inside... and then works its way out.

- Bob Moawad

Prize quality as a
precious gem.

- DeCarlo Eskridge

◆

Use what talents you possess; the woods would be very silent if no birds sang there except those that sang best.

- Henry Van Dyke

◆

We are hoarding
potentials so great
that they are just about
unimaginable.

- Jack Schwartz

♦

When you change the
way you look at things, the
things you look at change.

- Wayne Dyer

♦

The difference between a mountain and a molehill is your perspective.

- Al Neuharth

$\mathcal{M}$y advice is to go into something and stay with it until you like it. You can't like it until you obtain expertise in that work. And once you are an expert, it's a pleasure.

- Damon Richards

◆

$\mathcal{M}$y father always
told me,
"Find a job you love and
you'll never have to work
a day in your life."

- Jim Fox

◆

$\mathcal{M}$otivation is the art of getting people to do what you want them to do because they want to do it.

- Dwight D. Eisenhower

◆

Do what you feel in your heart to be right - for you'll be criticized anyway.

- Eleanor Roosevelt

Success is 99% failure.

- Soichiro Honda

◆

The better I get, the more
I realize how much better I
can get.

- Martina Navratilova

♦

$\mathcal{W}$e're all self employed sales people in the business of customer service.

- DeCarlo Eskridge

♦

You are what you repeatedly do. Excellence is not an event - it is a habit.

- Aristotle

♦

Stop selling. Start helping.

- Zig Ziglar

◆

Nothing in the world can take the place of persistence. Talent will not; nothing is more common than unsuccessful men with talent. Genius will not; unrewarded genius is almost a proverb. Education will not; the world is full of educated derelicts. Persistence and determination alone are omnipotent.

- Calvin Coolidge

♦

$\mathscr{I}$deal conversation must be an exchange of thought, and not, as many of those who worry most about their shortcomings believe, an eloquent exhibition of wit or oratory.

- Emily Post

♦

Of we had no winter, the spring would not be so pleasant: if we did not sometimes taste of adversity, prosperity would not be so welcome.

- Josh Billings

◆

$\mathcal{B}$eginning is not only a kind of action. It is also a frame of mind, a kind of work, an attitude, a consciousness.

- Edward Said

♦

People don't ask for facts in making up their minds. They would rather have one good, soul-satisfying emotion than a dozen facts.

- Robert Keith Leavitt

◆

Security is mostly a superstition. It does not exist in nature, nor do the children of men as a whole experience it. Avoiding danger is no safer in the long run than outright exposure. Life is a daring adventure or nothing at all.

- Helen Keller

♦

Sell your cleverness
and buy bewilderment.
Cleverness is mere
opinion. Bewilderment
brings intuitive knowledge.

- Jalal Uddin Rumi

Success is the culmination of failures, mistakes, false starts, confusion, and the determination to keep going anyway.

- Nick Gleason

$\mathcal{E}$very memorable act in the history of the world is a triumph of enthusiasm. Nothing great was ever achieved without it because it gives any challenge or any occupation, no matter how frightening or difficult, a new meaning. Without enthusiasm you are doomed to a life of mediocrity but with it you can accomplish miracles.

- Og Mandino

I believe Business Objects is on the cusp of becoming a multi-billion-dollar sales company. There is tremendous growth potential for business intelligence.

- Mark Shuttleworth

◆

$\mathscr{O}$n the past the publishers I've worked with have been extremely generous. And in almost every case, have been people who believed in the work rather than the sales and marketing.

- Peter Sotos

◆

*R*emember that it is not where you come from, or not even where you are; it is where you are going that matters most.

- Bo Bennett

♦

We are salesmen every day of our lives. We are selling our ideas, our plans, our enthusiasms to those with whom we come in contact.

- Charles Michael Schwab

About the Author

DeCarlo A. Eskridge is a spiritual life-coach/ trainer, host of Blogtalk Radio's "Live Your Greatness," motivational speaker, certified hypnotherapist, certified N.L.P. practitioner/ trainer, author, and minister. He is very proud to have authored and independently-published several books through his company NU DAE Enterprises where he serves as President and CEO.

A prolific teacher and encourager, DeCarlo A. Eskridge reads over 50 books a year, and listens to countless hours of audio programs. He is a Certified Life Coach through Franklin Covey and a motivational speaker who earned advanced honors at Toastmasters International. He is also an Ordained Minister with over 25 years of biblical study.

DeCarlo A. Eskridge has been imbued with an inexhaustible, unyielding, and unrelenting thirst and hunger for knowledge. His mission is to travel the globe teaching, empowering, inspiring, and transforming the lives of millions with the truths he has discovered in order that every person recognizes who he or she is, what he or she can accomplish, and that they live it!

GEMS MASTERY SERIES

NU DAE Enterprise Publications

DeCarloEskridge.com

ISBN-13: 978-1469912424
ISBN-10: 1469912422

www.ingramcontent.com/pod-product-compliance
Lightning Source LLC
Chambersburg PA
CBHW051317170526
45166CB00002B/575